WELCOME TO
SKULL
CANYON

PRESCOTT HILL

Welcome to Skull Canyon
(Pacemaker)

Prescott Hill
AR B.L.: 2.7
Points: 1.0

UG

GLOBE FEARON
Pearson Learning Group

The PACEMAKER BESTELLERS

Bestellers I

Diamonds in the Dirt
Night of the Kachina
The Verlaine Crossing
Silvabamba
The Money Game

Flight to Fear
The Time Trap
The Candy Man
Three Mile House
Dream of the Dead

Bestellers II

Black Beach
Crash Dive
Wind Over Stonehenge
Gypsy
Escape from Tomorrow

The Demeter Star
North to Oak Island
So Wild a Dream
Wet Fire
Tiger, Lion, Hawk

Bestellers III

Star Gold
Bad Moon
Jungle Jenny
Secret Spy
Little Big Top

The Animals
Counterfeit!
Night of Fire and Blood
Village of Vampires
I Died Here

Bestellers IV

Dares
Welcome to Skull Canyon
Blackbeard's Medal
Time's Reach
Trouble at Catskill Creek

The Cardiff Hill Mystery
Tomorrow's Child
Hong Kong Heat
Follow the Whales
A Changed Man

Cover and interior illustrator: Sarah Waldron

Copyright © 1988 by Pearson Education, Inc., publishing as Globe Fearon®, an imprint of Pearson Learning Group, 299 Jefferson Road, Parsippany, NJ 07054. All rights reserved. No part of this book may be reproduced or transmitted in any form or by any means, electronic or mechanical, including photocopying, recording, or by any information storage and retrieval system, without permission in writing from the publisher. For information regarding permission(s), write to Rights and Permissions Department.

ISBN 0-8224-5336-3
Printed in the United States of America
6 7 8 9 10   08 07 06 05 04

Globe
Fearon
Pearson Learning Group

1-800-321-3106
www.pearsonlearning.com

CONTENTS

1 WELCOME, STRANGER 1

2 OLD FRIENDS 7

3 A NEW TOWN 13

4 TROUBLE 21

5 GET OFF AND STAY OFF! 29

6 UP AGAINST IT 35

7 QUESTIONS 43

8 THE CAVE 49

9 A DAY'S WORK 55

10 MAIN STREET 59

11 GETTING THE STORY 67

CHAPTER 1

WELCOME, STRANGER

Jack Dade sat tall in the saddle. He turned and looked back at the mountains far behind him. It had been a hard ride. It was still dark when he'd broken camp that morning. Now the sun was high in the sky.

Dade wiped the back of his hand across his mouth. He must have already eaten five pounds of dust today. He had started west two weeks ago. From the very day he left Jefferson City, he'd been eating dust.

He guessed he was about a two hours' ride from Red Rock. "It's time for a little break, old girl," he said, swinging down from his horse.

"Take a good drink, Blazer. There's no telling when we'll get the next one."

He didn't have to speak twice. Blazer dropped her head and began to drink from the stream.

Dade took off his hat. He held it in the stream. When it was filled, he lifted it above his head. He let the water fall over him.

It splashed over his head and down his neck. It was cold. And it was good.

"This is more like it, Blazer," he said. "This is just what the doctor ordered."

He put his hat into the stream a second time. But as he lifted it, it was knocked from his hands.

A half second later, he heard the bang. It came from across the stream, to the left. He saw a little circle of smoke. It floated above a large red rock.

He thought it sounded like a Sharps buffalo rifle. He jumped to his feet.

"Go, Blazer!" he shouted. He hit her side with his hand. She took off running.

With a quick move, he reached for his holster. The pistol seemed to jump into his hand. He started firing and running.

He didn't aim. He just shot toward the circle of smoke as he headed for cover.

He saw a big log. It lay on the bank above his side of the stream. It must have washed up there in the spring. The summer sun had turned it white.

He jumped over it just in time. A bullet whispered right above his head. Then he heard the bark of the rifle. It was a close call. But he was safe—for now.

He lay on the ground, not moving. Then he took bullets from his pocket. As he slipped them into his Colt .44 six-shooter, he shook his head. This was some welcome.

He waited for a minute. Then he stuck his hat up above the log. Another bullet just missed it. It smashed into the log. Little bits of wood went flying. He listened hard to the sound of the rifle. He was sure now. It was a one-shot Sharps buffalo rifle.

He got to his feet fast.

The man with the rifle would be busy. It was time to move.

He left his hat by the log. The top of it just showed.

Then he ran across the stream. When he got to the other side, he ducked behind a pile of rocks. He was very near the big red rock. He watched it—and waited.

Soon, he saw the rifle stick out from behind it. There was another circle of smoke and another loud bang.

Back by the log, his hat went flying.

Now! He ran as fast as he could toward the red rock. When he got there, he circled it. He ended up behind the man with the rifle.

"Drop it!" he shouted. "Put your hands in the air!"

The man with the rifle looked up. Dade's pistol was pointed right at his head.

It was hard to tell how old he was. His hair was white as snow. Dade could see that he had spent his life outside. Cold winters and hot summers had weathered his face. Wind and sun had left their marks. He might be 50. He might be 80. Dade couldn't decide.

The man set the rifle down and shook his head. "You got the drop on me," he said. "But don't think I'm finished yet!"

"I don't think anything, old man," Dade said. "I just want to know why you were shooting at me."

The man's eyes flashed. "Because you work for Cleary."

"Cleary?" Dade said. "Who's that?"

The man looked surprised. "You don't work for Tom Cleary?"

"Never heard of him," Dade answered.

"Well I'll be!" the old man said. "What a mix-up!"

"Mix-up?" Dade said. He kept his gun pointed at the man. "You tried to kill me!"

"No! No!" the old man explained. "Not kill you. Just frighten you off. I thought you were one of Tom Cleary's men. I thought you were here to make more trouble."

Dade looked hard at the man's face. He couldn't say why, but for some reason he believed him.

"All right, old man," Dade said, "let's talk."

"Sure," the old man said. "But it would help if you put that away first."

"Okay," Dade said. He put his pistol in its holster. Then he reached out his hand. "My name is Jack Dade. People call me Dade."

The old man shook hands. "Howdy, Dade. My name is Sims—Clarence Sims. Most people call me 'Cactus.' You can call me anything you want. Just don't call me late for dinner."

"I won't, Cactus," Dade said with a smile. He wiped his hand across his mouth.

"Come to think of it," Cactus said, "it's already past lunchtime. Will you come to my ranch and let me feed you? Maybe I can make up for putting a bullet through your hat."

"Well," Dade said with a smile, "I'm hungry enough to eat a cow."

"That's not on the menu. But you're welcome to what I've got if you can stand my cooking."

Dade laughed. "I'll give it a try," he said. He put two fingers to his mouth and blew. Blazer heard the whistle. She came running, her head high.

"Just a minute," Cactus said. He led his horse out from behind a pile of rocks. "This here is Lazy Legs." He patted the neck of the little spotted horse. Then he climbed into the saddle. "Follow me," he said. The two men headed for Skull Canyon Ranch.

CHAPTER **2**

OLD FRIENDS

When Dade finished his second bowl of soup, he smiled. "That's good," he said. "I don't think I'll need that cow."

Cactus laughed and picked up his bowl. He put it to his mouth and drank from it. "Good to the last drop."

He set the bowl back on the table and looked at Dade. "Tell me," he said, "what brings you to this part of the country?"

"Just passing through," Dade said. "I'm headed west. But I have to stop in Red Rock. There should be a letter waiting for me there."

"With money in it, right?"

"I hope so," Dade said. He moved his soup bowl away. "Now," he said, "why don't you tell me about Tom Cleary?"

"Cleary!" Cactus said in a loud voice. "That rattlesnake!" He banged his fist on the table.

"He was once my best friend. But that was a long time ago. Now I don't even like to hear his name!"

"What happened?" Dade asked.

"Well," Cactus said, "it's like this. Tom Cleary and I grew up together. We were like brothers. We did everything together. Work. Play. Everything. Later on, we even owned a ranch together."

Cactus sat forward in his chair. He looked across the table into Dade's eyes. "Well, one day it all changed. A new schoolteacher came to Red Rock. Sarah Gray was her name. She was really pretty. Smart, too. Tom Cleary and I both took a liking to her."

A sad look came into his eyes. His voice grew softer. "To make a long story short, Tom Cleary won out. Sarah married him. I went my own way. I sold him my half of the ranch and started this one. That was about 25 years ago."

Cactus shook his head. "Last spring, Sarah suddenly took sick. They don't know what caused it. She died a week later. And then the trouble started."

"What kind of trouble?" Dade asked.

"First I found part of a fence torn down. Then someone shot one of my longhorns."

"Longhorns?" Dade said. "No one raises longhorns these days."

"You're right," Cactus said. "They all go for white-face cows now."

"Of course they do," Dade said. "The white-faced cows put on fat better. You really can't make any money on longhorns."

"I don't need the money. I already have enough. But I keep about 30 Texas longhorns for the fun of it. They help me remember the old days. They're mean and wild. Like me."

Dade smiled. He had worked Texas longhorns himself.

Cactus went on. "When Cleary started killing my cows, that did it. I kept my gun ready."

"Why would Cleary want to kill your cows?" Dade asked.

Cactus looked cross. "To trouble me. While Sarah was alive, we kept the peace. After she died, he tried to buy my ranch. But I wouldn't sell it. And now he thinks he can drive me off. He seems to think there isn't enough room around here for both of us."

Cactus banged his fist on the table again. "He may be right. But it won't be me who leaves!"

The old man's face had become red. "The real trouble started last week. When I was out riding, someone took a shot at me."

He looked hard at Dade. "That's why I tried to run you off. I thought you were one of them."

"It sounds bad," Dade said. "But are you sure that Cleary's to blame?"

Cactus got an angry look on his face. "What do you mean? Who do you *think* shot at me? Do you think I just made it all up?"

"Hold on there," Dade said. "I don't take well to being shouted at."

"Is that right?" Cactus said. He jumped to his feet. "Well, you had your lunch. Now you can just get out of my home! And off my land!"

Dade gave him a long look. He stood up. "Thanks for the food," he said. He turned and headed for the door.

As he rode off, he heard the old man's voice behind him. It was a loud shout. "And don't come back. Next time, it won't be your hat I'll shoot!"

"Let's go, Blazer," Dade said. "We don't need to take that kind of talk. Not even from an old goat."

CHAPTER 3
A NEW TOWN

It was late afternoon when Dade got to Red Rock. He looked for a stable. He found one on a side street. The sign said "Danny Flynn's Horse Care."

Dade liked the place. It looked clean. Danny Flynn was a giant of a man. Dade could see he had a way with horses.

"I'll be leaving Blazer for the night," Dade told Danny. He dug into his pocket. He found a coin and gave it to the big man. "Make sure she has feed and water."

Dade started out of the stable but stopped. Turning back to Danny, he said, "Is there a good hotel in town?"

"The Red Rock Hotel," Danny said. "It's supposed to be pretty good."

"If it's got a bed and bath, it's good enough for me."

"It's got that," Danny said. "It's at the end of Main Street. A big yellow place. You can't miss it. Are you staying long?"

"No, I'm just passing through," Dade said. "By the way, where's the post office?"

"Next to the hotel, in Peter Dawson's store. Pete's got just about anything you might need. He can pull your teeth, too."

Dade made a face. "No, thanks. Getting my mail will do." He headed for Dawson's.

It was dark in the store. Still, Dade could see all kinds of things for sale. There was everything from pots and pans to guns and bullets.

A fat man sat at a table. He was eating a big piece of pie. He looked up at Dade and nodded his head. Then he went back to his pie.

"Nice day," said a voice from behind.

"Howdy," Dade said turning. A thin bald man stood there. He wore a red bow tie over his white shirt. In his hand he held a broom. He was sweeping around the fat man's chair.

"Just cleaning up," the man said.

"Are you Mr. Dawson?" Dade asked.

"That's right," the bald man said. "Can I help you?"

"I was wondering if there might be any mail for me here."

"Could be. What's your name?"

"Oh, I'm sorry. My name is Dade. Jack Dade."

"Why, yes," Mr. Dawson said. "I think there *is* a letter for you. Just a minute."

He swept a pile of red dust into the street. Then he went to the back of the store. A blue hat hung from a nail on the wall. He put it on. He smiled at Dade. "U.S. Mail" was written on the front of it.

Mr. Dawson went over to a large desk. He took his time looking through a pile of mail. At last he took a letter from the pile. He held it up close to his eyes. Then he turned to Dade.

"What was that name again?"

"Jack Dade."

Mr. Dawson smiled. "John Dade?"

"That's right," Dade said. It was the letter he was looking for. The only person who called him "John" was his uncle.

When Mr. Dawson gave him the letter, Dade held it up to the light from the window. "Was there anything else?" he asked.

"No," Mr. Dawson said. "That's all."

Dade didn't look happy. "I was hoping for some money," he said.

He opened the letter. There was no check, just one sheet of note paper. It was bad news.

The letter said that business had not been good. His uncle was supposed to send him money. Now he might not be able to do so for another two weeks, if then. Dade put the letter away. He had only a few dollars left. There would be no bed and bath tonight.

"No money, I guess," Mr. Dawson said.

"No," Dade said. "Nothing."

Then a voice said, "Looking for work, cowboy?" It was the man who'd been eating the pie. But the pie was gone now.

"I guess I am," Dade said.

"Try the Double Diamond Ranch. I hear they need hands."

"Where's that?" Dade asked.

The fat man stood up. He was short. His feet were the smallest Dade had ever seen on a man. He walked over to the door. He pointed across the street to a barber shop. "The owner is getting his hair cut now. You can ask him."

"I'll do that," Dade said. He stuck out his hand. "Jack Dade's the name. I thank you for your help."

The fat man shook hands. "You're welcome," he said. "My name's Jason Harper. If you decide to stay around, come by and see me. I own the

Red Rock National Bank. It's a good safe place to keep your money."

"I'll remember that," Dade said, "if I ever get any money."

Dawson came over with his broom. Harper had left a trail of red dust. "Look out," Dawson said. He swept the dust out the door.

Dade thanked Harper again. Then he headed out the door. As he did, he bumped into a man coming in.

"Watch where you're going," he said to Dade. "Who do you think you are?"

"Sorry," Dade said. "I didn't see you."

The man was about 20 and was dressed in well-worn cowboy clothes. He seemed to be enjoying his own anger. "I guess you didn't, you fool!"

"Hold it," Dade said. "I told you I was sorry. There's no need for name calling."

"Is that right?" the cowboy said. "Well, *I'll* call you anything I want." He pulled back his arm and threw a punch at Dade.

Dade had done a lot of fighting in his time. But he had never learned to like it. With a quick step to the side, he ducked the punch. His own punch hit the man on the jaw.

The man didn't say a word as he dropped to the ground.

Dade got a good look at him. He was more a boy than a man, really. Dade shook his head. The young ones always want to fight.

"That was some punch."

Dade turned to see who was talking. Then he began to laugh. Half the man's face was white with shaving soap.

The man laughed, too. "I was getting a shave," he said. "I saw the fight out the window."

The man on the ground rubbed his jaw. He looked up at Dade and the other man.

"Get up, boy," the other man said. "We've got work to do."

He looked at Dade. "Can you take care of cows as well as you can fight?"

"When I have to," Dade said.

"Well, I need another hand," the man said. "I own the Double Diamond Ranch."

"I could use a job," Dade said. He stuck out his hand. "My name is Jack Dade."

The man took Dade's hand. "Mine is Tom Cleary." He pointed to the man Dade had punched. "This here is my son Jed."

CHAPTER **4**

TROUBLE

Dade stretched out on the bunk. He put his hands behind his head and closed his eyes.

He had been at the Double Diamond Ranch for a week now. But it had been several years since he last worked on a ranch. How many jobs had he held since then?

He had worked in a gold mine. He had driven a stagecoach. He had been a buffalo hunter for the army. He had even been a sheriff for a while in Texas.

And now he was back punching cows.

It would have to do for a while. When his money came, he would head west again. Maybe he'd go all the way to San Francisco. Perhaps he could start some kind of business there.

This train of thought was broken by a question from Jed Cleary.

"Say, Dade, can I ask you something?" Jed's bunk was next to Dade's.

Dade opened one eye. "Sure, Jed. What is it this time?"

Dade like Jed. The kid was a hothead, but Dade knew that would change. After their short fight, the two had become friends.

Dade had about 15 years on Jed. The young man stuck close to him. He watched everything Dade did. He asked a lot of questions.

This time Jed asked, "Will you teach me how to fight?"

Dade laughed. "I can tell you a few things, I guess. First off, don't pick fights. You'll get to see enough trouble. You don't have to go looking for it."

Jed rubbed his jaw. It no longer hurt from Dade's punch. He shook his head. "I know that now. But I want to learn about boxing. About trick punches and such."

Dade laughed. "Let me rest a bit. Tonight I'll give you a boxing lesson."

"Will you really?" Jed's face lit up in a smile.

"Yes," Dade said. "Now no more questions for a while, okay?"

Dade closed his eyes again, smiling. He liked the whole Cleary family—Jed, his big brother Billy, and Tom Cleary, too.

The father was a man of few words. He drove his men hard. But he worked as hard as any of them.

Dade had asked Jed about his father and Cactus Sims. Jed didn't know much. And brother Billy didn't know very much, either. Their father and Sims stayed away from each other. And Tom Cleary had told his men to keep clear of Skull Canyon. That was about all the two boys knew.

Dade himself had seen the bad side of Cactus Sims. The man got angry too fast. Dade couldn't blame Tom Cleary for keeping clear of old Cactus.

Well, Dade thought, it wasn't his business. He had other things to worry about.

Just then, he heard the ringing of iron on iron.

"Time to eat," Jed said.

Dade took out his watch. "It's a little early for the lunch bell," he said.

The bell kept ringing.

Finally Dade stood up.

Jed got up, too. Together with the other seven ranch hands, they headed for the big house.

Tom Cleary was coming out of it. He looked mad. "Who rang that bell?" he shouted.

"I did," said a short, round man dressed all in brown. It was Jason Harper, the banker.

"What's this all about, Harper?"

"Trouble." Harper said. "Big trouble."

"What is it?" Cleary asked.

"It's your son Billy. Somebody shot him in the back."

"Oh, no," Cleary said. "Is he . . . ?"

"Your boy is alive," Harper said. "But he's in bad shape. They took him to Doc Jones. Doc doesn't know if he'll come out of it or not."

"Who shot my brother?" Jed asked.

"We don't know for sure," the little man said. "I was in Red Rock when the stagecoach brought him in. The driver said he found him near Skull Canyon. I watched him while the driver went for Doc Jones. That's when Billy came to for a second."

"Did he say anything?" Tom Cleary asked.

"He just said one word, Tom. He said it over and over again."

"Well, what was it?" Cleary shouted.

Harper looked him in the eye. "*Cactus*," he said. "Billy just kept saying *cactus*."

The color went out of Tom Cleary's face. His mouth got a tight look. "Cactus Sims!" he said. He looked at his ranch hands. "Get your guns, boys! And get ready to ride."

Cleary started back into the big house. On the top step he turned. "Get my horse!" he shouted to Jed.

In a moment, Tom Cleary came back out of the house. He was wearing his six-gun. A fire seemed to burn in his eyes.

He climbed up into his saddle and spoke in a loud voice. "First, I'm going to town to see Billy," he said. "Then I'm riding for Skull Canyon." He looked at his men. They were already in their saddles. "Are you with me?"

By the sound of their shouting, it was clear that they were.

Striking his hat against his horse's side, Cleary cried out, "Let's ride!"

The Clearys were on the move.

The Double Diamond Ranch was almost an hour's ride from town. On the way in, Dade did some thinking.

Was it likely that Sims had ambushed Billy Cleary? Old Cactus was a hothead. But so were the Clearys. Dade knew something about how men acted. And he didn't think Cactus would shoot a man in the back.

Yet Harper had heard Billy say Cactus's name. It didn't make sense.

When they got to town, Doc Jones had some good news. Billy was sleeping. He had lost a lot of blood, but he would pull through.

While they waited for Billy to wake, Dade made up his mind. If Cactus Sims had shot Billy, he would have to be tried. But, Dade said to himself, that job belonged to the law. It did not belong to the Clearys.

Without saying anything to the others, Dade slipped out of the doctor's house.

A minute later he was in the saddle. "Let's go, Blazer," he said. He started out of town, riding hard for the Skull Canyon Ranch.

CHAPTER **5**

GET OFF AND STAY OFF!

Dade slowed Blazer when they were near the ranch house. He had tied a white cloth to a stick. He waved it in the air as he rode. Old Cactus would know enough not to shoot at a white flag.

Or at least Dade hoped he would.

Ten yards from the ranch house, he stopped.

Cactus stepped out the door. Held tight in his hands was his Sharps buffalo rifle. "What do *you* want?" he asked.

"I think you'd better hide out for a while."

"What?" Sims asked. His face got red. He brought the rifle up.

"Take it easy," Dade said. "I'm here to help you."

"Say what you have to say," Sims said. "And then get out."

"Someone ambushed Billy Cleary. Tom Cleary thinks you did it."

"Why, that . . . !"

"Hold on and listen!" Dade said. "I don't think you did it. But Tom Cleary does. He and his men are on their way here. And they don't mean to do you any good."

"Why, that . . . !"

"Save it for later!" Dade said. "You don't have much time."

"No one drives Cactus Sims off his land. Not today, tomorrow, or any other day. I'm staying!"

Dade shook his head. "Well, I thought that's what you'd say, Cactus. And I guess I'm going to stay here and help you." He got down from Blazer.

"You mean we'll fight together?" Cactus asked.

"No," Dade said. "I mean we'll try to *stop* a fight together." He turned toward the mouth of Skull Canyon.

A cloud of dust floated high in the air.

Sims looked at it. Cleary and his men were riding hard.

"All right, Dade," he said. "You got a plan?"

"Sort of," Dade said. "They have nine men. We have two. Still, it might work."

"Well," Sims said, "let's hear it."

A short while later, Tom Cleary brought his horse to a stop. He held up his hand. The men riding with him also stopped.

Cleary looked toward the ranch house.

"Come on out, Sims! You can't hide from me!" he shouted.

Cactus poked the end of his rifle out the door.

"Get off my land, Tom Cleary," said Cactus. "And stay off!"

"Not until I do what I have to do."

"You and your eight men, you mean."

Cleary got off his horse. He took a step toward the house.

"Never mind them," he said. "It comes down to just you and me. Man against man."

Cactus started to step out of the house. Then he stopped. He would give Dade's plan one chance.

"What do you want, Cleary?" Cactus said.

"You know what I want," Cleary said. "You shot my boy in the back. Let's see what you can do when a man is looking at you."

It was almost too much for Cactus. The heck with Dade's plan. Tom Cleary had gone too far! Cactus started to make a move.

Dade moved first.

He stepped out of the barn. As he did, he threw the rope. It was a good throw. It caught Jed Cleary clean. Dade pulled hard, and Jed fell from his horse. Dade rushed toward him and dropped down by his side.

Cleary's men turned. One drew his pistol and fired at Dade. The shot hit Dade's hand just as he was putting his right arm around Jed's neck.

Before the man could fire again, Tom Cleary grabbed him.

"Don't shoot! You might hit Jed!"

Cactus stepped out the door. He waved his rifle at the men. "All of you, put your guns away!"

Dade now had Jed in a tight hold. He held his pistol in his left hand.

"Listen, and listen good!" Dade said to Tom Cleary. "Jed stays put until you and your men are out of here. We don't want to hurt him. But if you cause trouble, anything could happen."

Tom Cleary looked at Dade with hate in his eyes. "I guess you were tied in with Sims all along," he said.

"Think what you like, Mr. Cleary," Dade said. "Just ride out of here. When I know you're far away, I'll let Jed go."

"Never mind me, Pa," Jed said. "Do what you have to do."

Tom Cleary looked at Jed. The boy was brave. He was a good son.

Cleary looked at Cactus and then at Dade.

"Don't think that this is the end of it," he said.

Dade started to say something. Then he stopped. He kept his gun on Jed. When Tom Cleary was out of sight, he put it away.

Dade looked at his right hand. It hurt, but he could stand it.

CHAPTER **6**

UP AGAINST IT

Dade held up his right hand while Cactus checked the bandage. It struck Dade funny. About six hours ago he had used that same white cloth as a flag. He had used it then to stop Cactus from shooting him.

Maybe he should have used it to stop Cleary's man from shooting at him, too.

Dade laughed, even though his hand hurt.

"I don't know why you're laughing," Cactus said. "You won't be able to use that hand for a week. Still, it should be okay. You're lucky. The bullet didn't break anything."

Jed sat in a chair across the room. His hands were tied behind him. He said nothing.

Cactus turned to Jed and said, "Son, you must be mad as a bear. Can't say I blame you. But there's no need to go hungry. I'll get you some food."

Jed shook his head.

"All right," Cactus said. "Have it your way."

He turned to Dade. "We don't have to keep him tied up, do we?"

"No, I guess not," Dade said.

Cactus took out his pocketknife and went over to Jed. He made two quick cuts. The rope dropped to the floor.

Jed still didn't say anything. But he nodded his head in thanks to Cactus.

The old man winked at him.

Dade pulled his chair up in front of the young man. "I want you to listen closely, Jed," he said. "Whether you believe it or not, Cactus didn't shoot Billy. But I think I know how you feel. Still, I had to do it. A lot of men could have been badly hurt."

Jed's mouth stayed closed.

Dade went on. "I want you to tell your father that Cactus is coming to town to see the sheriff. He'll be there the day after tomorrow. By then, people will be thinking clearly."

From deep in Skull Canyon came the scream of a mountain lion. When the sound died down, Dade said, "You can bunk here for the night. Ride out first thing in the morning."

Jed shook his head and stood up.

"It's a long ride in the dark, Jed. But it's up to you."

Dade handed him his gun. "I took the bullets, Jed. Be sure you tell your father what I said."

Jed headed for the door. Dade and Cactus followed him. Outside, the young man started toward his horse. The he stopped. He turned back to Dade. "I thought you were a friend," he said. "Now I know better."

Jed's horse was tied in front of the house. He climbed into the saddle. As he rode off, he shook his fist at Dade.

Dade went back inside. Cactus stayed out for a while. He watched until Jed was out of sight. Then he slowly walked back into the house.

Dade was over by the stove. He took some soup from a big pot. "Are you hungry?" he asked Cactus.

"No," the old man said. "I'll eat later."

Cactus took a chair by the fire. For a long time he was quietly lost in thought.

Dade watched him. He wondered what was on his mind. He guessed it had to do with young Jed Cleary. Then it hit him. Jed was Tom

Cleary's son. But he was also the son of Sarah Gray Cleary.

Tom Cleary hadn't been able to sleep at all. It was still dark when he heard the sound of the horse.

He ran out of the house. "Jed, is that you?" he shouted. "Are you all right?"

Jed got off his horse. "I'm fine, Pa, just fine. How's Billy?"

Tom Cleary smiled. "Billy's okay. They should be bringing him here today."

"Great!" Jed said.

"One thing, though," Tom Cleary said. "Billy doesn't remember what happened. He doesn't know who shot him."

"But I thought Mr. Harper said . . ."

"I know," Tom Cleary said. "But Billy can't remember saying anything about Cactus Sims. Don't forget, he was shot off his horse. Doc Jones said that when he fell he took a bad knock on his head."

"Then who *did* shoot him?"

"I *still* think Cactus Sims did it. But I can't say for sure."

Jed thought for a while. "You know something, Pa? It seemed to me that Cactus was acting all right."

"Maybe so," Tom Cleary said.

Jed then told him about Dade's plan.

"Why won't they see the sheriff today?" Cleary asked.

"Dade wants people to cool off," Jed said.

It made sense. But Tom Cleary wasn't happy. "It just might be a trick," he said. "I'll go along with it. But I'm not through with Cactus Sims. You can be sure of that."

And I'm not through with Dade, Jed thought. *You can be sure of that!*

Jed woke up to a shout from outside. "Here he comes!"

He jumped to his feet and rushed out. A cloud of dust was coming toward the Double Diamond Ranch. Tom Cleary stood in the yard. "It's Billy!" the father said with a big smile.

Soon, the two horses pulling the wagon stopped. Doc Jones was driving. Mr. Harper sat next to him. Billy lay down in the back.

Doc Jones smiled. "I brought you your boy."

Billy looked up at his father and brother. "Hello Pa . . . Jed." There was not much color in Billy's face. But there was a wide smile on it.

Jed and another ranch hand carried Billy inside. Doc Jones went with them.

"Wait," Harper said to Tom Cleary. "Could I have a word with you?"

"Why, sure."

Harper climbed down from the wagon.

He looked around before talking. His voice was soft. "Help is on the way," Harper said.

"What do you mean?" Tom Cleary asked.

"I sent for a man to go up against Dade."

"Dade?"

"Yes. I found out that Dade's a gunfighter. Sims, I think, is paying him. You have no chance against him."

"But . . ."

"You don't have to worry. I sent a telegram to Central City. Help is on the way."

"I still don't know what you mean."

"Does the name Simon Moon ring a bell?"

Cleary looked surprised. "The killer?"

"Call him that, if you like," Harper said. "But he always stays inside the law."

Cleary shook his head. "I won't pay money to a killer."

Harper smiled. He rubbed his hands together. "You don't have to. That's all taken care of."

Cleary started to say something. Harper held up his hand. "This Dade is bad for us all. His kind brings trouble."

"Yes, but what about Moon? What about *his* kind, Mr. Harper?"

"When his job is done, he'll go away." A smile showed on Harper's face. "Sometimes we just have to fight fire with fire."

"I don't like it," Cleary said. "My fight is with Cactus Sims."

"We can talk about that later." Harper smiled again. "Let's go in now and see your boy."

Cleary nodded and headed for the house.

CHAPTER 7

QUESTIONS

Dade woke up with a start. *What in the world is that noise!* he wondered. He sat up and looked around. Something *smelled* good. But something else sure *sounded* bad.

Over at the stove, Cactus was cooking bacon. He was also singing a cowboy song. He sang loudly and off key.

"Do I hear a coyote barking?" Dade asked.

Cactus turned around and laughed.

"Good morning," Dade said. He gave Cactus a funny look. "You're pretty bright and sunny today."

Dade pulled on his boots. Then he got up and walked across the room to sit down at the table.

Cactus cracked four eggs into the pan.

"Well," Cactus said, "I'm trying to make up for the way I've been acting. I guess I treated you pretty badly."

"Badly?" Dade said. "Why, no. Let's see. All you did was run me off your land. And try to shoot me a few times. I wouldn't say you acted badly. Not for a mad old goat like yourself."

"I guess I have to take that," Cactus said. "I had it coming to me."

"I won't kid you anymore," Dade said.

"That's fine with me," Cactus said. Then he added, "Dade, I've got to ask you something."

"Ask away," Dade said.

"How come you don't think I shot Billy Cleary?"

Dade's answer was to the point. "Because if you did, Billy would be dead now. You're a crack shot. And that rifle of yours could just about stop a train. The gun that shot Billy had nowhere near that power."

Cactus looked him in the eye. "You're pretty sharp," he said.

"And there's another reason you couldn't have done it," Dade said.

Cactus put his head to the side. "What might that be?"

Dade rubbed his hand across his jaw. "Because of how you felt about his mother, Sarah Gray. You would never hurt one of her sons."

Cactus spoke in a soft voice. "No, I wouldn't."

"Tomorrow, we have to make the sheriff believe that."

"Why wait?" Cactus asked. "Let's ride into town after breakfast. You explain it to the sheriff. Get this whole problem cleared up."

"It might not be so easy," Dade said. "Not until we find out who did shoot Billy."

"Well, how are we going to do that?"

Dade stood up and began to walk about the room. "We don't have much to go on," he said. "But let's start with Tom Cleary."

Cactus made a face.

"Never mind how you feel about him. When did you last talk with him?"

"You were there," Cactus answered.

"No," Dade said. "Before that."

"I thought I told you. I haven't said a word to Tom Cleary for close to 25 years."

"Wait a minute," Dade said. "I thought he tried to buy your ranch."

"He did. But he didn't come here himself. He sent someone else to do his dirty work. A little pig-faced banker."

"Jason Harper?" Dade asked.

"That's the one. Do you know him?"

"I've met him," Dade said. He thought back to yesterday. He remembered how Harper had stood in Cleary's yard ringing the bell. The first time they'd met had been in Dawson's store. Harper had aimed him toward the Double Diamond Ranch.

This was getting interesting. "So," Dade went on, "Tom Cleary has never been here. That is, as far as you know."

"Not for 25 years."

Dade rubbed his jaw again. "But *Harper* was here." He was talking more to himself than to Cactus.

"What has that got to do with anything?"

"I don't know," Dade said. He started toward the door. "You eat my eggs. And stay close to the house. I'll be gone for only a little while."

"Do you think Cleary will come back?"

"Not today, I don't. But this is far from over."

CHAPTER **8**

THE CAVE

Blazer stepped carefully, slowly picking her way along the trail. It had been a long day. She was getting very tired. Dade could tell by the sound she made as she took in air.

"Come on, girl," he said. He reached down and rubbed her chest. "It's time for a break."

He headed Blazer away from the canyon wall. When they reached the stream, he brought her to a stop.

"Easy, old girl," he said. He climbed down from the saddle. There was grass along the bank of the stream. He let the reins fall to the ground.

"You just take a rest," he said. "Have some dinner and cool off."

Blazer dropped her head toward the stream and drank.

Dade drank, too. Then he went over to a rock and sat down. It felt good to rest. The afternoon sun was going down. But it was still plenty hot.

As he got his second wind, his mind raced. He was looking for something. But what? That morning he had thought he would find an answer. Now it all seemed silly. Had he wasted a whole day?

Oh, well, he thought. There's no sense crying over spilled milk. He smiled at the sight of a baby bird. It seemed to dance about near the canyon wall. Then, just behind it, he noted something strange. There was a dead bush there that seemed out of place.

He got up and walked over to it. Someone had carried the bush there from the bank of the stream. When he pulled at it, he saw why.

It was being used to hide the mouth of a cave.

Dade had to bend low to see in. It was dark. But that presented no problem.

He went back to the stream. From his saddlebags, he got matches and a candle. A few minutes later, he was inside the cave. Once past the mouth, he could stand up.

It was cool inside. The walls of the cave were wet. Suddenly, as he took a step, his feet started to slide. The cave floor was covered with wet red clay.

He pressed against the wall to keep from falling. The candle dropped to the ground and went out.

He found it and lighted it again. And then he noticed the marks in the clay. Someone else had slipped there not long ago.

He held the candle close to the cave floor. The shoe print was small. It must have been left by a child. Or a woman. Or . . .

"Of course!" Dade said. He let out a shout of joy. "Well, I'll be a monkey's uncle!" he said. Then he almost slipped again but caught himself just in time.

The pieces were fitting together.

By the light of the candle he inspected the cave. It went back almost 20 feet. Here and there, a bright spark seemed to shine from the wall.

Dade set the candle on the cave floor. Then he took out his pocketknife. He opened it and pushed the end of it into a crack in the wall. He dug around for a while. Finally, he pulled out something thin and flat. He looked at it in the light from the candle.

He smiled. Then he folded the knife and put it away. He put the tiny piece he had cut out into his shirt pocket.

He didn't need to stay any longer. Stepping with care, he walked out of the cave. He put the bush back in place. Then he headed toward the stream.

It was dark when Dade returned to Cactus's ranch house. He had packed some bread and dried meat with him that morning. It had been gone by noon.

Tired and hungry though he now was, he felt great.

"Cactus," he said, "I think luck is with us."

"What does that mean?" Cactus asked.

"Warm me up some soup, first," Dade said. "Then I'll tell you the whole story."

"It had better be good," Cactus said.

"It's good," Dade said. "It's very good."

Later, Cactus decided that that wasn't the word for it.

"No," he told Dade, "*good* isn't strong enough. I'd say it's the *best* news I've heard in a long time. Maybe in my whole life!"

CHAPTER **9**

A DAY'S WORK

It was almost dark when the stagecoach from Central City pulled in. One man was there to meet it. He stood on the steps of the Red Rock Hotel.

"Hello, Mr. Harper," the driver said to him. "I'm running late today."

"Better late than never," the banker said. He made a dry little smile.

"I guess so," the driver said.

The guard sitting next to the driver reached behind him. "Watch out," he said to Harper. He threw the U.S. mailbag to the ground. Then he jumped down next to it.

"Red Rock!" the guard shouted. "End of the line." He opened the stagecoach door.

A tall, thin man stepped out. He was dressed all in black. His face was dead white. His dark eyes seemed to shine like black glass.

The man reached back into the coach for his bag. As his coat came open, a flash of white showed. The six-shooter in his holster had a bright bone handle.

Jason Harper took a step toward him. "Mr. Moon?" he asked.

The man in black looked down at the round-faced man before him.

"I'm Simon Moon," he said. His voice was deep.

"How nice to meet you, Mr. Moon," Harper said. He put out his fat little hand. "I'm the man who sent for you. Jason Harper."

Simon Moon took Harper's hand in his. "Hello, Mr. Harper," he said. He looked straight into the banker's eyes. "How long do you think this will take?"

"Oh," Harper said, "not long. You can probably leave on the noon stage tomorrow. I don't think it should take long at all."

Moon's right hand dropped to his holster. "I don't think so, either. One man should be just about a day's work."

Harper's mouth turned down a bit. "Well, Mr. Moon, there *has* been a small change."

"Change?" Moon said. He didn't seem pleased.

"Now," Harper said, "there's another man, too."

"Another man?"

"Please . . . don't worry. You'll be well paid."

Moon didn't answer right away. When he did, his voice was sharp. "The money's only part of it. The time is important, too."

"They'll both be together tomorrow," Harper said. "It should be easy."

"Easy?" Moon said. "Not these things. Fast, sometimes. But never easy."

Harper turned his eyes away. There was something about the way Moon looked at him. It made him feel uneasy. Almost afraid.

Moon spoke. "Do you have a room for me?"

"Oh, yes," Harper said. He turned toward the hotel. "Boy!" he called.

A boy with red hair popped out of the hotel. He ran down the steps two at a time.

Harper took the bag from Moon. He gave it to the boy. "Red, take this to room 23." He handed him a coin.

"Thank you, Mr. Harper," the boy said. He looked in his hand. The coin was a penny. He made a face. Then he carried the bag into the hotel.

Harper took Simon Moon by the arm. "First, Mr. Moon," he said, "let's stop by my office. We can get our business out of the way right now. I know you're not the kind of man who likes to waste time."

CHAPTER 10
MAIN STREET

Dade and Cactus got an early start. It was a fine morning. Blazer was well rested. So was Lazy Legs. Cactus's little horse had a real spring in his step.

The two men didn't talk much on the ride into Red Rock. They had said what they needed to say back at the ranch.

They hit town about nine o'clock.

As they rode down Main Street, Dade looked around. "That's strange," he said.

"What is?" Cactus asked.

"Where did everyone go?"

It was a good question. Main Street should have been busy by now. It was empty.

"Maybe they all went to church," Cactus said.

Dade gave Cactus a funny look. "On a Tuesday? All of them?"

"Oh. Well, no, I guess not," Cactus said. He rubbed the back of his neck. "I don't keep very good track of time out at the ranch."

Dade brought Blazer to a stop. He held out his hand. "This is far enough," he said. Cactus pulled up on Lazy Legs's reins.

Dade turned in his saddle. He looked up and down the street. He shook his head. There was worry showing on his face.

"Cactus," he said, "I think we need to get a plan together." He pressed his leg against Blazer's side. She turned and moved off toward the side street. Cactus and Lazy Legs followed.

Soon they were inside Danny Flynn's stable.

"Good morning, Danny," Dade said.

"Hello, Dade," the big man said. "I guessed I'd be seeing you today."

"Is that so?"

Danny nodded his head toward Cactus. "Everyone in town knows Cactus Sims is coming to see the sheriff."

"Word gets around fast," Dade said.

"That's right," Danny said. "The trouble is, the sheriff isn't here."

Dade looked surprised.

"No," Danny said. "He left town this morning. Told me he was going to Tom Cleary's."

"But Cleary is supposed to be here!" Cactus said.

"He is," Danny said. "He and his boys rode in about an hour ago. I hear they're down at the hotel talking to Harper and the new man."

"New man?" Dade asked. "What new man?"

Danny looked toward the back of the stable. "Come on out, Red!"

The boy from the hotel stepped forward.

"Go on," Danny said to him. "Tell Mr. Dade about the new man."

"Well," the boy began, "I knew he was a bad man right away. He was mean looking. He has a great big pistol with a bone handle. He . . . tied his holster to his leg. And . . . then I knew. I could see that he . . . he . . . ." The boy was tripping over his words.

Dade held up his hand. "Slow down, son!" he said. He climbed down from Blazer and handed Danny the reins. Then he picked the boy up and set him in the saddle.

"Just take your time," he said. "There's no need for you to rush."

The boy looked down at Dade. His face broke into a wide smile.

"Now," Dade said, "do you think you can tell me the man's name?"

"Yes, sir," the boy said. He was trying his best to speak slowly. "Mr. Harper got him a room under the name Jackson. But . . . but . . . ," he started to speed up.

Dade held up his hand.

The boy took a deep breath. He pushed out his chest a little. "But I saw his real name on his bag."

He looked at the three men, his eyes wide.

"Go on, boy," Dade said.

"His real name," the boy almost shouted, "is *Simon Moon!* The famous gunfighter!"

Cactus whistled softly.

"I thought you might want to know about that," Danny said.

"Thanks, Danny," Dade said. "And thank *you*, young man."

Dade lifted the boy and set him down on the ground. Then he took a silver dollar from his pocket and gave it to him. "You go get yourself some candy."

The boy's mouth dropped open. His eyes lit up with joy. It was a lot of money.

Dade felt it was well worth it.

There was no joy in Cactus's eyes. As he got down from Lazy Legs, his look was angry. "So," he said, "they sent Simon Moon after me."

Cactus took a small bag from his shirt pocket. It held bullets for his Sharps buffalo rifle.

"He's not after *you*," Dade said. With a quick move, he took the bag from Cactus's hand. "It's me he wants."

"Give me those back!" Cactus barked.

"Sorry," Dade said. He put the bag into his own shirt pocket.

The old man's face grew red. "What do you mean? If they want a fight, I'll give it to them!"

"No, Cactus," Dade said. "You wouldn't stand a chance against Moon."

"But . . ."

"No buts about it, Cactus. Moon is one of the best guns there is."

"The best, is he?" Cactus said. "Well, then, what makes *you* think you can go up against him?"

Dade dug around in his saddlebag. He came out with a rawhide string. "I didn't say he was *the* best."

Cactus watched as Dade tied his holster against his right leg.

"I know you're good," Cactus said. "But you won't be so fast with your paw all banged up."

Dade held up his left hand. "This one works just fine," he said. He opened and closed his fingers. "I'll use a cross-draw. I'll be a hair slow. But not much."

Dade turned the pistol around in the holster. The gun's handle now faced forward.

Cactus shook his head. "Oh, Dade, I don't like this one bit."

"I don't, either," Dade answered. "I wish there were another way. But I don't think there is."

He looked at Cactus. "You wait here. I've got to do this by myself."

"All right," Cactus said. But Cactus didn't put a lot of feeling into the words.

CHAPTER 11
GETTING THE STORY

Dade walked down the center of Main Street.

About a hundred feet behind him came Cactus. He kept to the side of the street. He hadn't listened to Dade.

Ahead, the street was empty. Along the way, people peeked out of windows.

Mr. Dawson stood in the doorway of his store. Dade nodded to him. He ducked back into the store.

At the end of Main Street, Dade stopped across from the Red Rock Hotel. He cupped his left hand to his mouth. "Simon Moon," he shouted, "come out!"

Dade waited in the empty street.

Suddenly the front door of the hotel opened. Through it stepped Moon, Harper, and Tom and Jed Cleary.

The Clearys and Harper stepped to the side. Moon came down the steps.

He moved out into the street, stopping about 20 feet up from Dade. He wore no coat. The handle of his pistol was bright white in the morning sun.

Dade stood facing Moon. He held his right hand behind his back. His left hand hung by his side.

Moon spoke first. "So, Dade, we finally meet. I've heard a lot about you. You're well known in Texas."

"I've heard about you, too," Dade said.

Moon smiled. It was a cold smile. "Shall we begin?" he said. He held his right hand away from his body.

"Wait!" Dade said. He held his left hand high. "I have something to say first."

Moon nodded. "Go on," he said, "say your piece."

Dade looked at Tom Cleary. "You and Cactus were friends once. Now you're both growing old. You can be friends once more."

"Are you a fool?" Cleary shouted. "He tried to kill my son!"

"No," Dade said. "Not Cactus." He looked Cleary hard in the eye. "Do you remember the gun Cactus always used?"

Cleary thought for a second. "Sure. That Sharps buffalo rifle was his favorite."

"It still is," Dade said. "But that's not the gun that shot your boy. If it had been, Billy would be a dead man now."

"Well then, who . . . ?" Tom Cleary started to say.

"The same man who found gold in Skull Canyon," Dade said. "The man who tried to buy Cactus out, using your name. The man who killed one of Cactus's longhorns and who shot at him. The man who set you two against each other. The man who tricked the sheriff into leaving town today . . . Jason Harper."

"You liar!" Harper shouted. He reached inside his coat. His hand came out gripping a small Derringer pistol. It was pointed right at Dade.

Just as Harper was about to pull the trigger, Jed Cleary stepped forward. With a quick move of his hand, he hit Harper's arm. The bullet went wide. It hit the sign on Dawson's store.

At the same time, Moon made his move.

Dade was ready.

His left hand whipped across his body. In the wink of an eye he had his pistol in his hand. He pulled the trigger once. There was a loud bang.

Simon Moon stepped back with a cry. His pistol dropped to the ground. He gripped his right arm with his left hand. He couldn't believe it.

Dade stepped toward him. He bent over and picked up Moon's pistol. He emptied the bullets out on the ground. Then he stuck it back into Moon's holster.

He looked at Moon's arm. "Doc Jones can look at that. The stagecoach leaves at noon. Be on it!"

Moon said nothing. He turned and walked toward Doc Jones's office.

Dawson rushed out of his store. He had a piece of rope in his hands. "Let's tie this critter up." He made a face at Harper. "We can lock him in the back of my store until the sheriff gets back. I just hope the rats can stand the company."

Jed quickly tied Harper's hands. "Let's go," he said, as he pushed him toward the store.

Dade looked at Cactus and Tom Cleary. "Now," he said, "you two shake hands."

Cactus stuck out his hand first. Cleary was quick to take it. "I guess we have a lot to talk about," he said.

Cactus laughed. "About 25 years to catch up on, I'd say."

Cleary turned to Dade. "Fill me in. How did you know it was Harper?"

"I didn't, at first," Dade said. "It came bit by bit. There was something fishy about Harper's visit to Cactus. He said that you wanted to buy Cactus's ranch, Tom. But it didn't seem you had any need for it. It's a good place for long-horns but not for anything else."

"That's for sure," Cactus broke in.

"And the story about Billy was strange, too. No one but Harper heard Billy say Cactus's name. Harper got away with his lie because Billy couldn't remember anything.

"The pieces didn't really fit together until yesterday. I was poking around in Skull Canyon and I came across an old mine out there. In the mine, I found this."

Dade reached into his shirt pocket. He took out a tiny, flat piece of gold. "There's a lot more where this came from," he said.

"I also found footprints in the mine. It was then that I remembered the first time I met Harper. It was in Peter Dawson's store. Dawson had been sweeping the place out. I noticed that Harper had dried red clay on his shoes. That same clay is on the floor of the Skull Canyon mine."

Dade rubbed his jaw with the back of his hand.

"Harper thought Tom would kill Cactus for killing Billy. When Billy didn't die, Harper decided he'd better come up with a new plan. That's when he sent for Moon."

"And Harper knew I didn't have any family," Cactus said.

"That's right," Dade said. "When you were dead, he'd be able to buy the land cheap. He was going to have Moon take care of me, too."

"How did he know about the mine?" Cleary asked.

"I don't know," Dade said. "As a banker, he may have come across an old claim. I guess that will come out at his trial."

Cactus laughed and banged his hands together. "You sure spoiled his plans!"

"Thank God," Tom Cleary said. "Well," he added, "I've got one more question."

He looked Dade in the eye. "Will you come work for me again?"

"Hold on!" Cactus said. "He works for me! He can run my mine."

"Wait, you two," Dade said. "Don't start fighting again."

Tom Cleary and Cactus looked at each other. They looked at Dade. Then all three men began to laugh.

Dade was still laughing when Dawson came out of the store. He pulled at Dade's arm.

"I forgot to tell you," he said. "This came for you last night." He handed Dade a letter.

Dade looked at the writing on it. He could tell it was from his uncle. As he opened the letter, a smile came to his face.

"This is a nice surprise," Dade said. He took out the check and read it. "It looks like I won't be working for either of you. I'm headed for San Francisco."

Dade put two fingers to his mouth and whistled. As though she'd been waiting for the sound, Blazer came running.

She looked fresh and lively. She looked ready to start the long trip west.